GIRL TALK

by

Dori Appel & Carolyn Myers

SAMUEL FRENCH, INC.
45 WEST 25TH STREET   NEW YORK 10010
7623 SUNSET BOULEVARD   HOLLYWOOD 90046
LONDON   *TORONTO*

Copyright © 1992 by Dori Appel and Carolyn Myers

ALL RIGHTS RESERVED

CAUTION: Professionals and amateurs are hereby warned that GIRL TALK is subject to a royalty. It is fully protected under the copyright laws of the United States of America, the British Commonwealth, including Canada, and all other countries of the Copyright Union. All rights, including professional, amateur, motion picture, recitation, lecturing, public reading, radio broadcasting, television, and the rights of translation into foreign languages are strictly reserved. In its present form the play is dedicated to the reading public only.

The amateur live stage performance rights to GIRL TALK are controlled exclusively by Samuel French, Inc., and royalty arrangements and licenses must be secured well in advance of presentation. PLEASE NOTE that amateur royalty fees are set upon application in accordance with your producing circumstances. When applying for a royalty quotation and license please give us the number of performances intended, dates of production, your seating capacity and admission fee. Royalties are payable one week before the opening performance of the play to Samuel French, Inc., at 45 W. 25th Street, New York, NY 10010; or at 7623 Sunset Blvd., Hollywood, CA 90046, or to Samuel French (Canada), Ltd., 80 Richmond Street East, Toronto, Ontario, Canada M5C 1P1.

Royalty of the required amount must be paid whether the play is presented for charity or gain and whether or not admission is charged.

Stock royalty quoted on application to Samuel French, Inc.

For all other rights than those stipulated above, apply to Samuel French, Inc.

Particular emphasis is laid on the question of amateur or professional readings, permission and terms for which must be secured in writing from Samuel French, Inc.

Copying from this book in whole or in part is strictly forbidden by law, and the right of performance is not transferable.

Whenever the play is produced the following notice must appear on all programs, printing and advertising for the play: "Produced by special arrangement with Samuel French, Inc."

Due authorship credit must be given on all programs, printing and advertising for the play.

ISBN 0 573 69327 7   Printed in U.S.A.

No one shall commit or authorize any act or omission by which the copyright of, or the right to copyright, this play may be impaired.

No one shall make any changes in this play for the purpose of production.

Publication of this play does not imply availability for performance. Both amateurs and professionals considering a production are *strongly* advised in their own interests to apply to Samuel French, Inc., for written permission before starting rehearsals, advertising, or booking a theatre.

No part of this book may be reproduced, stored in a retrieval system, or transmitted in any form, by any means, now known or yet to be invented, including mechanical, electronic, photocopying, recording, videotaping, or otherwise, without the prior written permission of the publisher.

IMPORTANT BILLING AND CREDIT REQUIREMENTS

All producers of GIRL TALK *must* give credit to the Authors of the Play in all programs distributed in connection with performances of the Play and in all instances in which the title of the Play appears for purposes of advertising, publicizing or otherwise exploiting the Play and/or a production. The names of the Authors *must* also appear on a separate line, on which no other name appears, immediately following the title, and *must* appear in size of type not less than fifty percent the size of the title type.

AUTHORS' NOTE

Girl Talk began with "Tick-Tock" and "Wobblies," which were written and performed for a week-long conference on relationships held at Southern Oregon State College. Because of the enthusiastic endorsement of audiences, and the response of so many that it was high time someone paid attention to friendships between women, we decided to expand the show to a full length production, considering women's friendships throughout the life cycle.

As we began, we were impressed at how neglected our subject had been, and how suspiciously regarded. Despite the importance of friendships in our own lives and those of most of the women we knew, the usual treatment in drama and literature was to portray relationships between women as trivial or hostile, and always incidental to those involving men. When considered at all, themes were frequently those of competition and treachery. Without ignoring or denying the negative attributes of any human relationships, we wanted to write about what our experience had taught us: that friendships between women were generally warm and supportive sources of personal understanding, common interests, shared humor, and affection. Like any other relationships, they changed over time, were often complex, and sometimes difficult.

So much for substance and content. As playwrights, we wanted to have a lively and original show, and being the particular playwrights we are, we wanted it to be both funny and emotionally affecting. Lots of laughs and some tears. At the end of four years of extensive touring, we were able to conclude that we had more than met our goal.

During the three productions of the show in our area alone (which is the home of several other theater companies, including the Oregon Shakespeare Festival) we found that we were often playing to "repeaters," who were back to see the show for a second or even third time. *Girl Talk* makes a very personal impact on people of both sexes, and because of these elements of recognition and identification, requires close attention to rapport with the audience.

In our own productions, we played all twelve roles ourselves, using a very simple technical plan which allowed us to change sets and costumes quickly, in direct view of the audience. In situations requiring a shortened format, we omitted the two historical pieces, "The Unmapped Way" and "Arrangements." On a few occasions, one or two scenes from *Girl Talk* were presented by themselves. Productions using a larger cast might choose a more elaborate technical approach, while maintaining the personal tone and immediacy essential to the play.

Girl Talk is a play of seven scenes, tracing women's friendships throughout the life cycle.

ACT I

Scene 1: Rites of Passage ....by Dori Appel
Scene 2: Grace Under Pressure ....by Carolyn Myers
Scene 3: The Unmapped Way ....by Carolyn Myers
Scene 4: Tick-Tock ....by Dori Appel

ACT II

Scene 1: True Stories ....by Dori Appel
Scene 2: Arrangements ....by Dori Appel
Scene 3: Wobblies ....by Carolyn Myers

NOTE: Casting is extremely flexible. The play can be performed with as few as two or as many as twelve actors. If performed by two, a single set and minimal costume changes enhance the connection between actors and audience. Two coat racks, positioned upstage right and left, enable the actors to change costumes and characters in full view. Shelves for props upstage center, and a table and two chairs downstage center are the only furniture required.

ACT I

Scene 1

Rites of Passage by Dori Appel

CHARACTERS

JENNY: A twelve-year-old girl. She is energetic, self-absorbed, and very focused on her budding physical development.

GEORGIE: Jenny's best friend, also twelve. She appears younger than Jenny, and is somewhat tomboyish in manner. She is conspicuously less than delighted by Jenny's important news.

TIME & PLACE

The present.
A private spot on school grounds.

SETTING: We are at the meeting place where Jenny and Georgie wait for each other during lunch hour.

AT RISE: JENNY is impatiently waiting for GEORGIE. SHE carries school books, and once or twice quickly checks herself in a hand mirror hidden inside her notebook. GEORGIE enters with schoolbooks, unaware of Jenny's urgency.

JENNY. I thought you'd never get here! Why are you so late?

GEORGIE. I had to stay after class for a make-up assignment. Miss Frisbie says my work is totally unacceptable. She says you have to be more than a jock to pass seventh grade science.

JENNY. Georgie, I got it!

GEORGIE. Just because I missed Tuesday for volleyball practice. Got what?

JENNY. *(Very excited.)* I got it!

GEORGIE. Jenny! You got volleyball captain? Oh, that's great! I knew you'd get it. It had to be me or you, we're the best! And I'll be co-captain, right? Like we promised.

JENNY. I don't mean that.

GEORGIE. You didn't get captain? Then who did?

JENNY. I don't know who did.

GEORGIE. Did Lisa? That's not fair. Everyone knows you and I are the best.

JENNY. Georgie!

GEORGIE. What?

JENNY. I GOT *IT*!

GEORGIE. How do you know?

JENNY. (*Sighs in exasperation.*) Georgie.

GEORGIE. When?

JENNY. This morning. I woke up and it was all over my pajamas. I mean all over! Even the sheets.

GEORGIE. Really?

JENNY. It looked like a war!

GEORGIE. Oh God, what did you do?

JENNY. I didn't know what to do! I couldn't leave my room because my father and my brother were having breakfast and I'd have to walk right by them, so I hollered, "Hey Mom, come quick!" And she yelled back, "Come out here, Jenny. I can't hear you!" I kept calling, "Quick! Quick!" and my father was shouting, "Your mother isn't your servant! If you want to talk to her, come out here!" And my brother was hollering, "Spoiled brat! Don't pay any attention to her!" And this went on for about an hour.

GEORGIE. You should have phoned me from your room. I would have brought you my sister's stuff. I could have smuggled it in in my lunch box.

JENNY. Finally my mom came and stood in the doorway and said, "Well, what is it?" I was so mad I held up the bloody sheet like a flag, and she gasped and ran out, with me standing there *dripping* blood.

GEORGIE. Oh, no! Did she tell your father?

JENNY. Of course not, it's private. She came back in a minute with a box of stuff—and then she slapped me.

GEORGIE. Slapped you?

JENNY. Not hard. It's a custom. Because I'm a woman now. It was only a love pat.

GEORGIE. Why should she slap you for being a woman?
JENNY. I told you, it was only a custom.
GEORGIE. If you are one.

(JENNY gives her a look and primps her hair.)

GEORGIE. You don't look any different.
JENNY. I don't? Really? I was sure everyone could tell. In home room Danny looked at me just as though he *knew*.
GEORGIE. Maybe he did.
JENNY. Oh my God! (*Twists to see her backside.*) Did anything come through? (*Looks down at her crotch.*) Can you see lines?
GEORGIE. *(Annoyed.)* No.
JENNY. You can't tell from there. Get down and look.
GEORGIE. (*Gets down on the floor.*) This is ridiculous!
JENNY. Modess Juniors are supposed to be guaranteed against showing lines. But you know, I don't think I have ever seen lines on anyone except Joyce Reardon, and that's only because she wears three on the first day.
GEORGIE. What does she do that for?
JENNY. On account of the *quantity*. Her cousin told me one time she had to have a transfusion because she lost so much blood.
GEORGIE. Oh, that's awful! Can't they stop it?
JENNY. I guess not. Well I'm sure that's a rare case. Joyce Reardon is a rare case anyway.
GEORGIE. What if that happens to you?
JENNY. It won't.
GEORGIE. But you said you were all covered with—

JENNY. My mom says it's a perfectly natural process. Like the tides.
GEORGIE. Tides?
JENNY. The *rhythm.*
GEORGIE. What are you talking about?
JENNY. And the seasons.

(GEORGIE looks blank.)

JENNY. You know, the sap flows into the branches in the spring, just like ...
GEORGIE. Like what? Plants don't *bleed.*
JENNY. No, but it's the same thing. The plants bud and flower—and so do we!
GEORGIE. Is that what your mother said?
JENNY. Sort of. I mean, the tides flow, and the moon ... The flowers open to the sun ... She got pretty sentimental. She was crying, actually.
GEORGIE. *Why*?
JENNY. Because it's a very special thing, becoming a woman.
GEORGIE. Will you stop saying that? You can't be a woman in the seventh grade unless you're retarded and have been there for a very long time. (*Looks closely at Jenny.*) You look kind of pale.
JENNY. Well, I feel terrific! And changed. I feel like a different person.
GEORGIE. You're just the same, except you're a little pale and you're talking weird.
JENNY. I guess it's hard to explain if you haven't—
GEORGIE. Well then don't bother. It's boring.
JENNY. (*Determined not to react to Georgie's insult.*)

Oh, I forgot. My mom's going to buy me that blue sweater we saw.

GEORGIE. (*Peering at Jenny.*) I guess now you'll get zits.

JENNY. The periwinkle one with the long sleeves. (*Touching her face.*) Everyone has a few.

GEORGIE. I don't.

JENNY. Well, you will. When you stop being a child.

GEORGIE. What?

JENNY. Nothing.

GEORGIE. Did you say when I—

JENNY. I told you it was nothing important. Look, did you see Danny staring at me in home room?

GEORGIE. No.

JENNY. Well, tomorrow notice, okay? And tell me after.

GEORGIE. If I think of it.

JENNY. Why are you being this way?

GEORGIE. What way?

JENNY. You know.

GEORGIE. Just because I don't want to hear about your blood-soaked pajamas and the tides and the moon and the flowers and—

JENNY. Look Georgie, it's not my fault I got it first.

GEORGIE. Who said it was?

JENNY. Well, you seem to be mad or something.

GEORGIE. It's boring, that's all. And I also don't see why you have to act so superior. It's not as though you *did* anything.

JENNY. I never said I did.

GEORGIE. Any cow can do it.

JENNY. Cows can't. We learned that in biology.

GEORGIE. Any horse then.

JENNY. They can't either.

GEORGIE. Well, any *dog*. Any poodle, collie, Pekinese ...

JENNY. No! They go into heat. It's different.

GEORGIE. You'll probably go into heat, too. That's probably why Danny was staring at you.

JENNY. Stop it!

GEORGIE. Well, he was. You said so yourself. He probably looked over at you and saw you were in heat—

JENNY. I'm not in heat!

GEORGIE. And the sap was flowing and flowering, and the moon was pulling all your tides out of you, and he probably took one look and said to himself, "She's got it, and now she's going to want to *do* it!"

JENNY. I don't either! You're just jealous.

GEORGIE. I suppose now you won't even be able to play volleyball.

JENNY. Of course I will. Why shouldn't I?

GEORGIE. Cramps.

JENNY. Don't you ever read *Seventeen*? Girls nowadays don't get cramps.

GEORGIE. My sister does. Bad ones. She has to stay in bed all day.

JENNY. Well, your sister ...

GEORGIE. Don't say anything about my sister!

JENNY. I thought you hated her.

GEORGIE. Just don't.

(There is a pause.)

JENNY. Georgie?
GEORGIE. What?

JENNY. You can borrow my blue sweater when I get it.

GEORGIE. No thanks. I might catch what you've got.

JENNY. Don't you wish! Well, *don't* borrow it then. I don't care. (*SHE starts to gather up her things to leave.*)

GEORGIE. You really wouldn't mind? When it's brand new?

JENNY. You're my best friend! (*Pause.*) But you do have to wear deodorant so you don't stink it up under the arms.

GEORGIE. I'll have to get some.

JENNY. Then get some. *(Pause.)* You don't mind my telling you, do you?

GEORGIE. (*Unconvincingly.*) 'Course not.

JENNY. Aw, c'mon, Georgie ... I just meant it ... you know. Woman to woman.

End of Scene 1

ACT I

Scene 2

Grace Under Pressure by Carolyn Myers

CHARACTERS

GRACE: A slightly disheveled, agitated, well-read feminist, around thirty years old. SHE has a sense of humor.

TIME & PLACE

The present.
The living room of Grace's house.

SETTING: Grace's living room in the late afternoon. There is a small table set for tea, with pot, cup, sugar bowl and creamer, which do not necessarily match. On the table are also a pad of paper, a recently crumpled note, a pen and, most important, a telephone.

AT RISE: GRACE is seated at the table, preparing herself a nice cup of tea. SHE has just read a note from her husband, stating that he has left her. SHE is composed and civilized as SHE addresses the audience.

GRACE. This is a very macho act. It is! I learned this from reading Ernest Hemingway. It's called "grace under pressure." You see, I can sit here calmly, (*SHE begins pouring the tea.*) having a lovely cup of tea all by myself even though my husband and my best friend have run off together. (*SHE notices that the cup is overflowing.*) My husband and my best friend! AUGGHHH! I feel like a cartoon! (*SHE attempts to mop up the spilled tea, then gives up.*) You know, when I first learned about feminism, it was like a religious revelation for me. It was! It even had all these mantras, you know, slogans you can repeat again and again—"The personal is political," "Take back the night," "I am woman." My personal favorite has always been "Sisterhood is powerful." And it is! I knew sisterhood was powerful, I had all my feminist causes, I had my women's group, and I had Vivian. Vivian is my best friend. The one who is with my husband, David, right now in some motel somewhere fucking their brains out. I wonder if she's bored. I wonder where her kids are. We live right down the block from each other, we have total child care exchange. I would think the child care alone would keep her from such a rash act. Some of you out there must have children under five. Tell me truthfully, what would you choose—endless, guilt-free child care, or sex? Really, there's no comparison.

I want to call Vivian. I can't believe she would run off and have an affair without telling me first. I feel so left out. No, of course, what am I thinking of? She couldn't call *me*, I'm her lover's wife. (*GRACE looks longingly at the phone.*) And I mustn't call her, I mustn't. Still, Vivian is so great to talk to, she has such perspective on all my problems. Maybe she would be able to put her personal involvement aside for a few minutes, and listen to me. Yes, I'm certain she could do that. She's very mature. (*SHE starts to dial, then slams down the phone.*) No. What am I doing? I'm nuts. I am!

In *Ms.* magazine they once said that one difference between men and women—you know how we feminists love to find differences between men and women—We do! Anyway, one difference, according to *Ms.*, is that in a moment of crisis women always know exactly who they would call, while men aren't sure. I believe that. I know who I would call—Vivian! Only now I can't. I now understand the real crisis when your husband and your best friend run off together is not losing your husband, it's losing your best friend!

If only David had done this with someone else, right now I could be a basket case on the couch there, freaked out and speeded up, panicked. Vivian would bring all her kids over to spend the night, and we would sit up all night figuring out what in hell I was going to do, and trashing David, and defending David, and crying and laughing about how weird life is! But now all I can do is sit here and think about Vivian.

Maybe I should call someone else. One of my other friends in the women's group. No, there's simply no one else around here of Vivian's caliber. There's not! Now if I were in London I could call up Doris Lessing. She's an intelligent woman. (*SHE looks at phone.*)

Oh, what the hell, why not? (*SHE dials.*) Yes. London. Lessing, Doris or D. (*SHE places her hand over the receiver and speaks to the audience.*) I love the way the English talk. They make everything sound so important! (*Speaking to the phone with British accent.*) Yes, yes, got it. Cheerio! (*SHE redials.*) Hello, Doris? Doris Lessing? Oh, speak to me, Doris. Out of the many fractured hues of women's experience, teach me! Vivian and David have run off together! (*Pause.*) Ahhh, yes I see—(*SHE repeats what Doris has said.*) The split I feel is mirrored exactly in global dimensions in the struggle of minority races and developing nations, microcosmed psychologically by schizophrenic episodes, psychically through the Sufic intuitive realms, and in the world of physics through quarks. (*Pause.*) Thank you, Doris. (*SHE hangs up phone and addresses audience.*) It's as I always suspected, Doris Lessing is too intelligent for me. I need a soul mate. I do! (*SHE dials.*) Overseas operator? Edith Piaf please. (*To audience.*) She's dead? Don't worry. This phone has all the new options. (*To phone, with slightly French accent or affect.*) Hello? Bonjour? Edith? Oh Edith, my little friend. Ma petite amie. My little wounded bird. Let me walk the streets at night with you, Edith. The gutters of Paris are filled with beautiful abandoned women, Edith, but we will be together, singing the joys of unfettered existence, the rights of the vagabond. (*To audience.*) Mon dieu! Oh no! I'm getting Edith Piaf mixed up with Colette. I am! (*SHE hangs up.*)

I better stick to America. Emily Dickinson! (*SHE starts to dial.*) At least I can do her some good. If she'd had a best friend she might have published in her lifetime. (*SHE stops dialing and hangs up.*) The truth is, I'm afraid to call Emily Dickinson. I am!

I'm afraid that having a best friend might ruin her, hold her back. Emily Dickinson, Joan of Arc, the Virgin Mary, can you imagine any of them having a best friend? "Don't listen to him, Mary, they all think they're God." And then where would we be? We wouldn't have Jesus!

But that's not the way it is. It's not! Vivian didn't hold me back. She encouraged me to be bold. So great, now I'm sitting here all bold and she's run off with my husband. Hey, this is progress. I'm starting to feel a little anger here. Seize the time!

(*SHE dials.*) Hello? Bonjourno? Is this fifteenth century Italy? Good. Lucretia Borgia, please. Lucretia, darling, your poison ring, your secret recipes. Seduction, Lucretia! Seduction and betrayal! I hates her, I hates her forever!

But I don't. Not yet. Right now I just miss her. I don't understand. Why did she pick David? He's so unworthy of her. Have you ever noticed how your best friends, male or female, always pick lovers who aren't good enough for them? But in this case, the difference is extreme, believe me. And she knows David, too, she knows everything about him. For example, David is obsessed with skin care. He has a lotion, a potion, an oil, or a cream for every inch of his body. At one point he was using ten different external body care products simultaneously. He was! Vivian didn't believe me, so I bet her a back rub and she hid in the laundry hamper and watched him. Now, could you have an affair with a man after you saw him do something like that? Vivian did give me a great back rub though.

(GRACE pauses as revelation strikes.)

Wait a minute! That's it! Oh, oh, I see it all now. How could I have been so blind? Vivian is in love with me! This fling with David is just transference. I read all about it in *Psychology Today*. I should have seduced her. Obviously. But how? I am completely unversed in these matters. (*SHE looks at phone.*) To the source! *(SHE dials.)* Sappho? Oh, Sappho, my wandering shepherdess, woman of words and song, let me breathe your honeyed breath as night winds— *(SHE hangs up.)* No. Forget it. We just weren't friends like that.

(The PHONE rings.)

What? Oh God, who is it? It's them! I know it's them, what will I say? *(SHE picks up the receiver.)* Hello. David! Where are you, David? I've been so worried. Note? Oh, yes, of course I got your note. *(SHE picks up note from the table.)* Right, I know you're leaving me. How's Vivian? Oh, yes, I know it's hard for her too. (*Pause.*) She'll have to leave her job? What job? Vivian doesn't have a job. (*Pause.*) And she wants me to know that she really respects me? *Respects* me? David, what have you done to my

Vivian to make her start talking like that? (*To audience.*) He's laughing! (*To phone.*) No, not *my* Vivian, that chicken dumpling? (*To audience.*) Chicken dumpling? I resent that! (*To phone.*) You're there with Vivian *Burnett,* Ryan's teacher? Oh no! Listen David, can you call me back? In about an hour, okay? Don't do anything I wouldn't do. Bye.

(SHE hangs up and feverishly redials. To phone.)

    Vivian. Oh, Vivian, Vivian, I am so sorry! I love you. How could I ever doubt you? Why haven't you called me? The line was busy? Oh, yeah. Vivian, you have to come over right now. The most terrible thing has happened. David's left me! Yes! With Ryan's teacher, can you believe it? Come right now! I'll leave the door unlocked, I'm going to have a psychotic episode on the couch. Bring the kids for all night, stop by Safeway and buy a bottle of Burgundy and ice cream ... no, a quart, at least a quart! Oh, Vivian, Vivian, Vivian, sisterhood is powerful! It is! *(SHE raises phone receiver in victory salute.)*

End of Scene 2

ACT I

Scene 3

The Unmapped Way by Carolyn Myers

NOTE: Mabel Reed and Mary Arnold are historical characters. They wrote memoirs of their adventures in California in the early twentieth century, which were published under the title *In the Land of the Grasshopper Song*. This fictional scene draws on those memoirs, but takes place after the years covered in that account.

CHARACTERS

MABEL REED: An unmarried Philadelphia lady, about twenty-four years old. Mabel is sturdy, adventurous, and chaffing at the bonds which she feels Philadelphia society places upon her.

MARY ENDICOTT ARNOLD: Mabel's best friend, also in her mid-twenties. Mary is a young society matron. She is a wife, a mother of young children, an artist, and an embracer of life, both past and present.

TIME & PLACE

The spring of 1915.
Mary Arnold's studio, in the attic of her lovely Philadelphia home.

SETTING: We are in Mary's attic painting studio. Included in the furnishings are a covered painting, a shelf of memorabilia, and a table and chair. Cut flowers and a vase are on the table.

AT RISE: A party is about to begin downstairs. MARY is arranging flowers for decorations, as MABEL sneaks in. MABEL brings their collaborative diary, and has about her an air of secret news.

MABEL (*Entering.*) Boo!

(*THEY embrace.*)

MABEL. I told you I wouldn't be late. Here I am, ten minutes early for your party.
MARY. Will wonders never cease!
MABEL. And ready as I'll ever be to meet Philadelphia society. Oh, and I brought the journal. (*SHE holds it out.*)
MARY. (*Takes the journal and crosses to a chair and sits.*) Our brilliant collaborative effort. Let me see. Of course, everyone will want to hear all about our journey. What exotics we are in this little world. (*SHE picks up journal and begins to read.*) "In 1909 we got our assignments from the Bureau of Indian Affairs and, over the outraged protests of family and friends, we crossed the country by rail to San Francisco, thence to Eureka. We took a stage to the mountains, proceeded by horseback and then by burro, only to be stopped, in our last mile, by the most perilous footbridge one could ever imagine. For a

long moment we just stood looking at it."

MABEL. I shut my eyes and prayed. Papa Frame tried to reassure us.

MARY. (*As Papa Frame.*) "It's not so bad, once you get used to it." (*SHE mimes stepping on the bridge.*)

MABEL. I stepped on. The bridge moved, up and down, and swayed a little.

MARY. "You got to keep your balance, that's all."

MABEL. (*Continues her remembered walk across the bridge.*) I didn't dare look down at the river, very far below me. I kept my eyes on the cliff ahead, put one foot down, lifted it, tried to keep my balance, rested my weight on it, and lifted the other foot.

MARY. "Just keep your balance."

MABEL. Every time I took a step the bridge swayed.

MARY. "Used to be handrails, but they're kinda sagged. Wouldn't advise you to use 'em."

MABEL. Crossing a bridge like this is nothing to make a fuss about. If it wasn't so far up in the air, and the bridge only kept still, why it would be nothing at all.

MARY. "Don't look down if the river bothers you. Put your foot down when the bridge goes down, and just keep a-going."

MABEL. Heaven knows I don't want to stop. Don't look down, don't look down. Just watch the cliff.

MARY. "That's right. You can't plan ahead on a bridge like this. You just got to keep a-going."

(*As Papa Frame, SHE pretends to help MABEL off the bridge and then returns to being herself.*)

MARY. But you get used to things in that country.

MABEL. Panthers and rattlesnakes and bridges.

MARY. We got so we hardly noticed it. And then, one day, you had gone on ahead. *(SHE reads from the journal.)* "I followed, riding the big horse, Baby, thinking nothing in particular until we reached the center of the span."

(During the following description, MABEL and MARY sometimes share the story with the audience.)

MABEL. I heard a sharp crashing sound.

MARY. "The bridge where I had been was gone, and Baby and I were hanging in mid air, astride a beam. Baby's middle rested on the beam and her feet dangled down over the bottom of the gorge, far, far below. The saddle started to slip around, my feet were tangled in the stirrups, we were going to fall. I thought I would just pray and die." Then I heard your sharp voice.

MABEL. Pull the cinch strap, the cinch strap!

MARY. "I pulled that strap as we all fell headlong into the gorge. Me, the saddle, and Baby. But the saddle fell clear. By the time I came up for air, Mabel had rushed down the gorge, by the side of the river, and was pulling me out."

MABEL. And we found Baby, not dead as we had expected, but limping toward us. A fall with you and the saddle would have broken her back.

MARY. And incidentally drowned me. As it was, I only broke my leg.

MABEL. As it was, under such conditions, it was a miracle that you were alive.

MARY. "Getting home was not easy. We were only about eight miles from Kot-e-meen but the trail seemed endless."

MABEL. Poor Baby was so lame that she could hardly move one leg after the other. And black night was upon us, and there were still miles to go.

MARY. And you were carrying me. And leading Baby.

MABEL. I never ceased to hate night on the trail. We forded creeks in the thick blackness, to the soft gurgling sound of unseen water. It was so dark I had to feel my way along, stumbling over stones and rough places and trying to make out the trail with my feet.

MARY. With every mile poor Baby limped along more slowly. I fainted from the pain.

MABEL. When at last we came out on the high ridge above our own valley, and could see far below us the dim outline of O-we, our mountain, I wept with relief.

MARY. I opened my eyes. It was my resurrection.

(SHE puts down the journal and retrieves the painting. From this point the scene becomes a realistic conversation between the two characters.)

MABEL. Oh Mary, it's perfect, perfect!
MARY. It's the view from the top of the ridge.
MABEL. Our mountain!
MARY. I got the bend in the river, didn't I? Finally. Yes.

(MABEL reaches for the painting.)

MARY. But you can't have it yet.
MABEL. Why not? You've been promising me for so long.

MARY. There's a smudge right there.

MABEL. Where? Mary, that smudge is invisible to the naked eye.

MARY. And I haven't got the water right yet. The painting has to be perfect. I never thanked you for saving my life.

MABEL. You can't thank someone for crossing the river. It isn't done.

MARY. No, it's not polite. And you can't brag either. The only proper Indian response is to joke.

MABEL. Do you think that you're still a bit Indian, Mary, from living with the Essie family for two years?

MARY. A bit. Like right now, I'm Indian. I know you've come to say something to me. I've got the sense. Oh, Jeremy hates me to say it, but I do. I've got the sense. Well, when it comes to you anyway. And you're a bit Indian, too. So we stand here, and I know you have something to say, and you're in no hurry to declare it. How long will I have to wait, Mabel?

MABEL. I'm going back.

MARY. Mabel!

MABEL. I got my assignment today from the Bureau of Indian Affairs. This time I'm supposedly a schoolmarm! But I'll be all the way up the river, way past Happy Camp. They shouldn't be able to watch me too closely all the way up there.

MARY. You can't leave Philadelphia.

MABEL. I've got a two-year contract for the start. I'm leaving next month.

MARY. No. You can't just up and go back. We can never go back. Remember when we rode out to Arcata? We looked back and the mountains had closed behind us.

We were white women again, in a white man's world.

MABEL. Yes, much to our astonishment. We were down below. And you said, the way you felt then, we might as well have fallen in Siuslaw Creek and never gotten out.

MARY. It was fabulous in the mountains, dear. I know. No one else will ever know. We fooled them all. But we were young, foolish, wild—

MABEL. You sound like my mother.

MARY. Maybe I do. Mabel, we were very, very lucky. You know that. Somesbar was practically wiped out in a flood last year, and Essie's daughter, Asypanee, was mauled by a panther in our very own cabin!

MABEL. And Sarah Quincy's daughter was run over by a carriage in downtown Philadelphia!

MARY. It's different, Mabel. Admit it. We had the luck of youth with us then, we didn't even stop to think. We weren't responsible like now.

MABEL. You're the one with responsibilities.

MARY. What about your parents?

MABEL. They've other, much better daughters.

MARY. What about Phillip?

MABEL. Phillip is only a friend, always.

MARY. And me.

MABEL. Yes, there is you.

MARY. Yes, what about me? What am I supposed to do without you? I can't ... I know this is unfair. But I can't bear it.

MABEL. You have so many friends, Mary.

MARY. But I love you more than any of them. And I can't talk to Jeremy. He's frightened of everything I have to say. I can only love him.

MABEL. Mary, don't.

MARY. What have I got to lose? You're going. Fine, I'll go too. I'll say goodbye to all of them. Watch me. I'm going with you, Mabel.

MABEL. But the children.

MARY. Yes. The moment Sara was born, the very first moment I laid eyes on her, I didn't feel love, I felt trapped. I said to myself, "Here it is, Mary Endicott Arnold, you have finally committed an irrevocable act." That whole year after we came back from California, the Klamath River raced inside me. And then, in that one moment, when I first saw my first baby, it stopped. Dammed up. And from then on, that girl I used to be, who traveled on horseback, and climbed cliffs, and found heron nests, and stayed up all night with sick Indian women, that girl was dammed up too. And I was trapped in this small life, a young Philadelphia matron of good social standing. Me!

MABEL. I know. I'm always living on the Klamath in my mind. Just this evening, getting ready for your party, I was remembering when we moved into our cabin. We were a little set back because we had no cloths to scrub with. One of a thousand things you couldn't buy in that country. But your pioneer ancestors came through.

MARY. I think they flourished about two hundred years ago, dear.

MABEL. That doesn't matter. The genetic strain is still there. For an hour, you walked about, looking inward. And then you suddenly went out, chose a spot seemingly at random, and started digging. You dug up a pair of old coveralls that had been buried behind a pepper bush who knows how many years before. I never knew how you did that.

MARY. And we had no furniture.

MABEL. We were eating and sleeping on the floor. When we had our first party, our friends sat on the woodpile, and Doctor Kilfield brought us lice and flea dip for a present, and Essie brought us dried eels.

MARY. (*SHE shudders involuntarily.*) Oh, stop.

MABEL. What?

MARY. We were so dirty!

MABEL. Yes. But we were happy.

MARY. Don't look at me like that, Mabel. I didn't say we weren't happy. I just appreciate being clean.

MABEL. Here we're so spic and span that very few occupations are open to us. I'm always living in the past with you, Mary. I'm riding horseback with you next to the Klamath, shouting to you over the noise of the rapids and then I blink my eyes and I'm sitting in your parlor having tea, or I'm at dinner, watching you with your husband and children, and you know you love them, Mary—

MARY. Yes, I do.

MABEL. Or I'm going home alone after some festive holiday.

MARY. Mabel, move in with us. We've asked you before. The children adore you. Jeremy ...

MABEL. Would tolerate me.

MARY. Oh no, you know he—

(*Pause. THEY regard each other.*)

MARY. ...would tolerate you.

MABEL. Staying here for you isn't enough. We aren't friends like we were in the old days. We were always doing something then, and now all we have to talk about is old times. I'm an odd bird, Mary, those years on the Klamath changed me. I can't be a Philadelphia lady.

MARY. Of course you could, if you wanted to.

MABEL. And I don't want to be your family's maiden aunt. Not yet, anyway. I'm not forgetting the invitation though. It sounds like a nice old age.

MARY. You're hardly the old maid type. Don't you want to get married?

MABEL. I don't know.

MARY. How about Reed McMannis?

MABEL. He is very attractive.

MARY. (*SHE begins chanting and dancing.*)

Ay-ah kuni a yah
Ay-ah kuni a yah
I-to poo-a-rum
Ee caro puh mooch.

MABEL. What are you doing?

MARY. Ay-ah kuni kuni ah yah. Don't you recognize this? It's Essie's love song. Not a plain, ordinary love song, but a true love charm, and it is warranted to bring down any gentleman you have your heart set on no matter how great his disinclination.

MABEL. Ahh, but you also have to drop a few grains of dirt from a special anthill in his coffee.

MARY. No trouble. (*SHE holds up a little bag.*) The deed is done.

MABEL. Mary!

MARY. Very valuable knowledge, Essie considered it, for unmarried ladies like ourselves. It was an heirloom in her family and very few Indians knew about it. Any young lady would gladly pay a large sum of money for it. But for you, I will give it as a gift.

MABEL. Essie said she could not have gotten Mart without it.

MARY. And I could not have gotten Jeremy.

MABEL. You didn't!

MARY. Indeed. And now I will descend the stairs to my party, greet my guests, and bring down Reed McMannis. How perfect! He lives next door.

MABEL. Mary, I forbid you.

MARY. Honestly, Mabel, don't you want to get married at all?

MABEL. Every time I think of marriage I remember poor Mrs. Petersen sitting in Yreka, waiting for her husband to come from wherever he was and take her up the river. Always waiting. I couldn't wait on a man like that, Mary. I just couldn't.

MARY. But if you were going back with a man I'd feel so much better.

MABEL. Why? We were happy, very happy, living in San Francisco that year after we left the river. But when you met Jeremy and wanted to move back to Philadelphia, everyone was so happy for you. Even I approved. I followed you back here. I knew I would miss living with you, but I felt that you were doing the right thing, choosing marriage and family. It's expected, getting married. Even though it broke up our home.

MARY. Oh, Mabel, *please*.

MABEL. Now, hear me out. If I were getting married, to a man from the Rivers say, and moving back for that, you would still feel sad. But you wouldn't try to stop me, like you are now, would you?

MARY. Probably not.

MABEL. But I'd still be gone three thousand miles. So

why is this so much less acceptable? If it helps you to pretend there's a man involved, pretend I'm moving back to marry Papa Frame!

MARY. I can't pretend that. Aren't you frightened to be going back all alone?

MABEL. I don't care about that. But I'll be without you, Mary. And that's what I don't know if I can stand.

MARY. I don't know either. And you're going soon?

MABEL. I'm going to Washington, D.C. next week.

MARY. I'll have your painting fixed by then.

MABEL. It is perfect.

MARY. Too bad about the smudge.

MABEL. Paint me there.

MARY. What?

MABEL. Yes, that's it. Paint me right there.

MARY. You'd be tiny.

MABEL. That's all right. Just paint me as a little red dot. Standing there in that red Indian shirt you made me. And then you keep the painting.

MARY. But it's yours!

MABEL. I'll be there, Mary. I don't need it anymore. Don't you see? I'll be right there. And every day, dear, come rain, snow or whatever, I'll go stand there at sunset, and I'll call to you. Indian style. With my mind. Don't cry.

MARY. I can't bear to think ahead.

MABEL. Don't think ahead then. Let's go down to the party and have a good time.

MARY. (*In Papa Frame's voice.*) "Sometimes, girls, you just can't plan ahead, you put one foot down and then the other. Keep your balance, that's all."

MARY and MABEL. "Just keep a-going."

End of Scene 3

ACT I

Scene 4

Tick-Tock by Dori Appel

CHARACTERS

JUDY: A woman thirty-six years old. She seems depressed and has a "space-y," distracted manner. She is given to self dramatizing and fanciful imagery.

LIZ: Judy's best friend, a little older. She is sensible and practical in manner, and obviously used to being Judy's helpful support, though we can imagine their roles being reversed on another day.

TIME & PLACE

The present, late morning on a Saturday in spring.
The kitchen of Judy's house.

SETTING: We are in Judy's attractive but somewhat cluttered and eccentric kitchen. Important furnishings include a table and two chairs. There are a coffee pot and two mugs on the table. (Coffee is drunk and mugs are refilled as needed throughout the scene.)

AT RISE: JUDY is seated at the table, drinking a cup of coffee as LIZ rushes in, breathless and concerned.

    LIZ. Judy?
    JUDY. (*Weakly.*) Hi, Liz.
    LIZ. I came right over. What's wrong?

(JUDY does not answer.)

    LIZ. Judy?
    JUDY. Nothing. Everything. I don't know.
    LIZ. Are you pre-menstrual?
    JUDY. No, I'm *mid*-menstrual! (*SHE starts to cry.*)
    LIZ. Mid-menstrual?
    JUDY. I'm ovulating!
    LIZ. Well, just don't do anything foolish in the next twenty-four hours and you'll be fine. How do you know? I never know.
    JUDY. I felt it.
    LIZ. Really? What does it feel like?
    JUDY. Kind of a ping.
    LIZ. A ping. You can hear it?
    JUDY. Not exactly. I was just sitting here having coffee

and wondering why Sylvia Plath didn't just go to a nice warm hotel and take pills instead of sticking her head in the oven in that miserable cold London flat, and I felt it go ping. It was number two hundred and seventy-nine.

LIZ. Number ...

JUDY. Two hundred seventy-nine.

LIZ. *(Pause.)* I was about to ask how you could know such a thing, but I guess you could figure it out.

JUDY. You don't even need a calculator. I got my first period just a month after my thirteenth birthday, and it's now four months after my thirty-sixth birthday, and so that's twelve times twenty-three years, plus three months more—two hundred seventy-nine!

LIZ. I would need a calculator. Why were you thinking about Sylvia Plath?

JUDY. Because she was so vain and self-centered and tragic. But she was gifted, too. That's why she could get away with it. If I stuck my head in the oven, no one would say, "What a shame, she was so brilliant, and she had only begun to do her really important work." I don't have any important work.

LIZ. Of course you do.

JUDY. If I died tomorrow, everyone would feel bad for about an hour, and then my boss would just move someone else into my office and life would go on. Writing copy for the Fruit-of-the-Month Club is not important work.

LIZ. Well, it's as important as what most people do.

JUDY. What's that supposed to mean? And it's dishonest besides.

LIZ. How can it be dishonest? You say the pears are good, the apples are good, and the—kiwis are good. And they are.

JUDY. I don't mean that. Look, Liz, I sit there writing dialogue for Harry and David, and there's a picture of them on the wall, smiling in their checkered shirts, and they look so easy-going and happy, and you can just imagine what a neat friendship they have, and how they go fishing on the weekends, and have Thanksgiving with each other's families so it's all like one big family, and they probably live just over the hill from each other, so their kids can walk down together to wait for the school bus, and it's all a total and complete Norman Rockwell *orgy*! But the truth is, Harry and David are dead! There is no Harry and David.

LIZ. Really? They're dead? I always thought ...

JUDY. *(Prompting her.)* ... that they ...

LIZ. ... lived next door to each other, and rolled up their checkered sleeves to pack up the pears, while their wives made jelly—oh, what does it matter? I don't care about Harry and David! Why are you being so morbid, anyway? I was having a perfectly pleasant morning making potholders—

JUDY. You were doing what?

LIZ. And finger puppets. Lyndon's school is having a benefit, and I promised I'd make something.

JUDY. For this you need a Masters in medieval history?

LIZ. What difference does it make? And if you want to know, I like making finger puppets.

JUDY. Maybe it's just as well I don't have kids.

LIZ. I made a rabbit and a lion and an old woman with curly gray hair—I used poodle cloth for the hair. And I give them really expressive faces. I mean, after I've been working on one it really seems alive!

JUDY. Like Harry and David.

LIZ. What did you call me over for, anyway?

JUDY. Just to talk.

LIZ. To talk. You phone me to come quick, it's an emergency. And hang up. And that's just to talk?

JUDY. I haven't had much time with you lately. Ever since you started seeing Stanley.

LIZ. I know, we've both been busy. What do you want to talk about?

JUDY. (*Shrugs.*) Just talk. I've been thinking of changing my name.

LIZ. What's wrong with your name?

JUDY. It's a kid's name. Why don't parents think of that?

LIZ. All right, so be Judith. Anything else on your mind?

JUDY. Will you remember to call me that?

LIZ. No.

JUDY. You see! Marilyn Monroe changed her name from Norma Jean. *She* was thirty-six when she died, just like I am, and she didn't have kids either. Sylvia Plath had kids. But Marilyn was beautiful. (*Beat.*) I think it's great that you didn't give Lyndon a baby name.

LIZ. Thank you.

JUDY. How did you happen to give him that name?

LIZ. You know perfectly well! You just want me to have to say one more time that it was Tom's choice, so you can ask me if it was a family name, and I'll have to confess that Tom admired Lyndon Johnson and wanted to name the baby after him, and then you'll hoot and laugh and tell me that was certainly grounds for divorce, and I'll remind you that I did, indeed, divorce him. Though not for that. Or not only for that.

GIRL TALK

JUDY. I'm sorry, I'm being a bitch.

LIZ. Yes, you are. Why?

JUDY. I'm envious.

LIZ. Of what?

JUDY. You. Your life.

LIZ. What's so hot about my life? I'm a single mother eking it out on totally inadequate child support and a stupid job that makes your ad copy for Fruit-of-the-Month look like being the poet laureate for the state of Oregon, and I'm spending my precious free morning while my son visits his newly married father in what used to be my house—

JUDY. —Oh, Liz, your house. How did you ever let that happen?

LIZ. You know how it happened. I got screwed on the divorce settlement, and I couldn't make the payments, so Tom very kindly took it off my hands for a sum that—Oh, you know all this! We've gone over it a hundred times. And, as I was saying, I was spending a rare free morning making goddamn potholders—

JUDY. You said you liked it.

LIZ. I like the finger puppets. I hate the potholders. They're so round and stupid, or square and stupid. I hate them!

JUDY. I'm sorry. Really I am.

LIZ. It's okay. We all have bad days.

JUDY. It sounds like you were having a reasonably good one until I called.

LIZ. And you still haven't told me why you did.

JUDY. I got scared.

LIZ. (*Showing concern.*) Did you get another phone call?

JUDY. No, my obscene caller hasn't phoned in nearly a

month. I almost miss him. He was the closest thing I've had to a suitor in ages. Liz, I'm a spinster!

LIZ. A what?

JUDY. I am. I am an unmarried lady of thirty-six years, and if that's not a spinster I don't know my Jane Austen or my Emily Brontë or—

LIZ. Your Gloria Steinem.

JUDY. It's not funny. At least you've been married.

LIZ. What difference does that make? I'm not married now.

JUDY. But you've done it. And you are seeing Stanley. And you have Lyndon no matter what.

LIZ. Lyndon is a terrific kid, I have to admit. Though men might not run so fast in the other direction if—

JUDY. He's running?

LIZ. No, not exactly.

JUDY. You are lucky, Liz. You and Lyndon are family.

LIZ. Not exactly the one I envisioned as a romantic teenager.

JUDY. Can I tell you why I called, what scared me?

LIZ. I've been kind of hoping you would.

JUDY. My parents called last night.

LIZ. Uh-oh.

JUDY. And as usual they asked what men I'm seeing, and I said Carl—(*LIZ snorts.*) which is true, and my mother started getting very eager, and said, "Oh, you've been seeing a lot of Carl." And I told her, "No more than usual." And she said, "Judy, darling, is it serious?" And I got mad and reminded her that Carl is gay, and she said, without skipping a beat—just a little disappointed, "Oh, still gay."

LIZ. Well, parents never give up.

JUDY. No, but I have. After I hung up I started feeling so guilty about how much they want grandchildren, and how I'm an only child and it's up to me to keep the line from dying out—

LIZ. What a marvelously archaic idea.

JUDY. Oh, I know it's silly, but that's how I felt. I saw all my genes—a bit disorganized, but interesting—just going down the tubes, you should pardon the expression.

LIZ. Judy—

JUDY. Liz, all night I couldn't sleep. I just lay there with my eyes wide open, listening to my biological clock. I could actually hear it ticking away. Liz, I'm thirty-six years old. In four years I'll be forty. That means I've only got that much time in which to find someone halfway reasonable, and get through all the relationship garbage enough to get married, and then work out all the marriage freak-out stuff enough to get pregnant, and even then I'll have to have amniocentesis, and I might still be carrying a mongoloid after all.

LIZ. Judy, do you really *want* to get married and have children?

JUDY. How should I know? I've never done it. (*With a quizzical look, SHE touches her lower abdomen.*) Oh God, there's another one.

LIZ. What?

JUDY. It went ping again. I think I just lost twins.

LIZ. I think you're losing your marbles. Promise me you'll be very careful for the next day or so.

JUDY. I'm perfectly safe. My caller hasn't phoned for a month, and my only plans for the weekend are dinner tomorrow with Carl, who seems to have no inclination whatever to save my family line.

LIZ. You don't have plans for today?

(JUDY shakes her head no.)

LIZ. I don't either.
JUDY. You're not seeing Stanley tonight?
LIZ. No.
JUDY. Liz, something's wrong! Why didn't you tell me?
LIZ. I had my hand on the phone when you called.
JUDY. What happened?
LIZ. You won't believe it.
JUDY. Tell me.
LIZ. He insisted that I have Lyndon circumcised.
JUDY. But Lyndon is ten years old!
LIZ. That's what I told him.
JUDY. It's crazy.
LIZ. I told him that, too.
JUDY. Well, thank God you found out now.
LIZ. I suppose.
JUDY. Liz, do men have our kinds of problems?
LIZ. They must, but they're different. It's harder to count sperm, for one thing. And clitoridectomies aren't fashionable right now—though I really can't imagine any woman insisting that someone's daughter—
JUDY. Oh, Liz, what'll we do?
LIZ. I don't know. Put our heads in the oven?
JUDY. We can't, it's electric.
LIZ. I don't have any other ideas.
JUDY. That was *my* idea, in case you don't remember.
LIZ. Right.
JUDY. There must be something else to do. (*Pause.*)

Why don't we do girl things?

LIZ. Like what?

JUDY. Lunch out at a nice place. And shopping.

LIZ. Shopping? Could we really do shopping?

JUDY. Of course, that's what girls are supposed to do.

LIZ. And manicures. I want to do manicures.

JUDY. Yes, manicures! Fancy ones, silk-wraps!

LIZ. And then cocktails, with our packages spilling all over the empty chairs at the table, and our gorgeous nails wrapped around the stems of our glasses!

JUDY. Oh, what fun! What fun! (*SHE looks disconcerted and touches her abdomen.*)

LIZ. Another ping?

JUDY. Yes, but I don't care. I couldn't *possibly* deal with triplets.

LIZ. You're absolutely right. And we're going to have a perfectly smashing afternoon. But Judy, darling ...

JUDY. Yes, darling?

LIZ. Wouldn't it be great if we had hats?

END OF ACT I

ACT II

Scene 1

True Stories by Dori Appel

CHARACTERS

LEILA: A woman almost forty-seven years old. SHE is graceful, intelligent, and humorous, and her present concerns should be presented as an unusual disruption to a generally confident and secure sense of self.

TIME & PLACE

The present.
Leila's living room or study.

SETTING: Leila's comfortable and attractive living room or study. Essential furnishings include a desk or table and chair. The desk top holds books and papers, one or two small, attractive art objects, and a vase of flowers.

AT RISE: LEILA is standing near her desk, studying herself in a hand mirror. SHE looks up and addresses the audience.

LEILA. I shouldn't even look in the mirror anymore. All I see is *wreckage.* If I could put my make-up on without looking, I would. But I have to tell you, this is a new preoccupation. I'm going to be forty-seven next week, and until a year or so ago I never thought about aging. All those magazine ads and Phyllis Diller jokes—that had nothing to do with me. Over the hill at thirty—what was that? (*Pause.*) Thirty. I married Gabe when I was twenty-four, and by the time I was thirty I had two toddlers, and Gabe was teaching at the college, and we had our own house and great friends, and I used to look at myself in the mirror and say, "Leila, you are in your prime."

Every morning I'd take the kids to the park, and Joanie and Syb would be there, too, and we'd sit together on the benches while the kids played, or stand next to each other while we pushed the swings and talked. Oh, I know what you're thinking—housewives at the park or in their kitchens, exchanging dopey small talk, their heads empty of anything more significant than a new recipe for sponge cake. But it wasn't like that. Syb and Joanie and me, we had real things to talk about. We were all active in the peace movement back then, and Syb was an artist—a serious painter and a good one.

(*Remembering.*) One time, and this was absolutely typical, we were over at Syb's, and all of a sudden she said, "This isn't my body." Just like that. Joanie and I looked at her for a moment, but Syb insisted. "It isn't. Carla, that girl who's been modeling for me, she's got my body, my real body. That's why I want to paint her."

Now if Syb had told that to the wrong people, she could have ended up on the back ward somewhere, waiting her turn for shock treatment. But fortunately, she told us, and we understood right away.

"Oh, Syb," I said, "people feel that way all the time, but they just don't say it, except in books. I've got a bunch of novels I could loan you—Toni Morrison, Cynthia Ozick, Anais—." I stopped because Joanie was giving me a look. She used to say I loaned books the way doctors prescribed pills.

"Syb," I said, "I'm sure Carla does have your body in some way, and that's why your painting is going to be so wonderful!"

Then Joanie looked kind of spaced, the way she does when she's about to utter something totally profound, and said, "That's the way I feel about my cat. Not his body, but *him*. When he goes out at night, he gets transformed right in the doorway, and he becomes so sleek and feral, and— it's *me*. He partly does it for my benefit, of course, to help me sleep. Knowing he's out there, so quiet and swift and merciless, I sleep like a lamb all night."

Joanie's husband left her when their daughter was three, and back then, when we were in our early thirties, she was going to school part time to finish her degree and get a teaching credential, and I was taking a Masters in lit., which was just legitimizing what I like to do best anyway. When I was a kid, my mother always used to say, "There goes Leila again, escaping into a book." It was partly true, of course, but I was also finding out how to get along when things got tough. When I read all those stories—like *The Secret Garden*—how Mary cured herself and Colin with Dicken's wonderful inspiration—it gave me a secret garden within myself, a green place that I can still return to in hard times.

For my thesis I was comparing the themes in women's novels to—. Oh, what does that matter? That was a long time ago. The point is that Syb and Joanie and I were not just dumb housewi—. (*Pause.*) The real point is that we were friends and we shared our lives. We were mothers together, sure, but it was way more than our kids. Joanie had boyfriends, who ranged from marvelous to deplorable, depending often on how long she knew them. And Syb and I had marriages, and you know that isn't the stuff of sitcoms. When you're with someone a long time, things are complicated. You can be really hurt or lonely—even desperate. So there I'd be, handing out prescriptions for them or for myself: "Try a little Margaret Drabble. Margaret Atwood. Grace Paley." (*SHE sighs.*)

What do men do when they're feeling down? They don't talk about it, at least Gabe and Syb's husband Peter never did. They're good friends, but I'm sure they've never talked about anything more personal than their jobs or their favorite teams, or what kind of insulation they're putting in the attic. When times were hard between Gabe and me, I think I would have died if I didn't have Syb and Joanie to talk to. We were on the same wave length, whether we were talking about our men, or just about ourselves—about who we *were,* and what we needed, and how hard it was sometimes to even know that, much less ask or insist on it.

Sometimes there were jealousies and conflicts among the three of us. And we were *awful* at knowing how to deal with them, I mean really terrible. So there were periods during those years when I didn't see one or the other of them for awhile. But eventually—and sometimes it took months—we got back together because we were the funniest and most interesting people we knew. And because we had shared so much for such a long time. I mean, you had to trust someone quite a lot to trash your own kids with them.

Once, when all of us had teenagers, and the little bastards were really pretty hard to take, we got together one evening at Joanie's house when her daughter Rhonda was out on a date. We had a bottle of wine, and pretty soon we got totally hilarious imagining ways to get rid of them all. We were all three pretty tipsy, and Syb said, "Maybe I could send the boys to a military school run by neo-Nazis. Just for a couple of years to teach them respect." Which got me wondering if my girls would catch on if I sweetly suggested a mother and daughter wilderness camping trip. When we got way out to the end of nowhere, I'd slip them each a Mickey in their bedtime hot chocolate, and then just leave them there fast asleep. Bye-bye, kids, it's been fun. But Joanie's plan was the most deliciously diabolical— sticking holes in Rhonda's diaphragm with a pin, so the kid would get pregnant and have to marry her boyfriend Billy, who Joanie figured wasn't really a bad sort for seventeen—not too bright, but good-tempered. Syb wasn't so sure.

"Joanie," she said, "it could backfire. *You* could get stuck with raising your *grandchild* for the next eighteen years."

"And what if you got caught?" I asked her. "It would be so embarrassing to have Rhonda find you with the pin in one hand and her diaphragm in the other—."

And in the middle of all this, in walks Rhonda! Who takes one look at her mother, smashed out of her gourd with dear old Aunt Syb and dear old Aunt Leila, and becomes seriously irate.

"Do you have any idea how you *look*?" she demanded, and that set us off even more.

"How do we look? Tell us!"

We were half-collapsed on the table, giggling hysterically.

"Just exactly what is so funny?" Rhonda fumed, with her hands on her cute little hips, like she was the parent and we were the kids. And naturally we couldn't tell her that her dear mother and the two loving ladies she'd known since babyhood were hatching this truly evil plan about her and the other darling children, so we just kept laughing until finally she stalked off to her room in disgust. And we still couldn't stop! I laughed so hard I peed in my pants, I honestly did! And we weren't in the least bit guilty. It was so much fun to be *planning* awful things happening to our kids instead of worrying and worrying about all the dreadful possibilities, the way we usually did. (*Pause*.) That was only three or four years ago.

Last year Joanie and I both had kids at college, and Syb had one son making out his applications—and another who'd dropped out of high school the previous year because of an intense love affair with cocaine and booze. Well, that's life. At least these days. And she still had two good friends to talk to. The fact was, though, she talked less and less about her son Adam, until finally she didn't talk about him at all. We didn't see much of her anymore. She was always busy with her painting—or just busy. I missed her, but there had been times like that before. Sometimes you need to be private, you need *not* to talk for awhile, and you need your friends to understand that and back off. So that's what we were doing when all of a sudden, out of the blue, Joanie announces that she's moving away! Ever since Rhonda went off to college, she'd realized that she wasn't tied to this pathetic little burg anymore—those were her words—and she was going back to Boston.

"Joanie," I told her, "Boston isn't the place you left twenty years ago. You can't even open the door to trick-or-treaters on Halloween."

"What novel did you read that in?" she wanted to know.

"This is the warning of a concerned friend," I said, but it didn't slow down her packing any. (*Pause.*) Now, I know this sounds silly, but I wasn't just sad at Joanie's leaving. I was shocked! People move all the time, I know, but I still couldn't believe it. When the new people moved into Joanie's house, I nearly called the cops. It was as though strangers were camping out in the middle of my own house. In the middle of my life.

Even long distance, though, I have more contact with Joanie than I do with Syb. That's true. Whatever we had for such a long time, we don't have anymore, and I don't know why. We never judged Adam or compared our kids with hers. Being mothers together, that was great, but like I said, it wasn't the most important thing. It was just that we were there with each other for such a long time. And the three of us, we're still the same people, aren't we? We care about the things we always did, and we have our work. Well, they do. I've got my books.

You know, I never did finish my Master's degree. Those years I just couldn't seem to get around to writing my thesis. I kept reading more and more women novelists, but I never *wrote* anything. The reading was what seemed important, that and talking about the ones I liked with Syb and Joanie.

Honestly, when I think about going through menopause without those two, I could actually scream! I mean, when the last little egg has gone its merry way, and I never, never again have to worry about getting pregnant, who am I going to bitch to about hot flashes? Who am I going to make jokes with about estrogen deficiency?

I look in the mirror and I seem to be sagging. Not just my face and body, but the self that lives inside. I need something to look forward to, so I've decided to write my thesis finally, and get my degree. I want to write about friendships between women in twentieth century literature, even though there isn't much to write about. In this instance, my sources have failed me. Friendships between females get about as much notice in literature as they do anywhere else.

But you and I, we know the truth, don't we? It's an old, old story and it hasn't changed. Throughout history, women have always had their best friends who they ran to see when their husbands went off to kill people, or their kids got stoned, or they found out they were pregnant again. It's the story of women bonded together over the years—like Syb and Joanie and me—piecing the fabric of our lives together like the thousand scraps of some lumpy, colorful quilt.

End of Scene 1

ACT II

Scene 2

Arrangements by Dori Appel

CHARACTERS

GERTRUDE STEIN: In her sixties. She is confident, expansive and optimistic, and clearly used to leaving all practical details to Alice, whom she clearly adores.

ALICE B. TOKLAS: Also in her sixties. She is considerably smaller in stature than Gertrude, somewhat fussy, quietly vigilant, and has a slightly acerbic wit. She clearly adores Gertrude.

TIME & PLACE

1944, shortly after the liberation of Paris.
Gertrude and Alice's Paris apartment at 5 Rue Christine.

SETTING: *We are in the drawing room of Gertrude and Alice's apartment. Since the two have just returned from their war-time exile in Culoz, the room is still rather disorganized, and shows signs of having been plundered by the Germans during the occupation. Books and some household articles are stacked on the table. Some paintings have been re-hung, however, including Picasso's famous portrait of Gertrude. Essential furnishings include an easy chair for Gertrude and a table or desk and chair for Alice.*

AT RISE: *GERTRUDE pauses in her pleased inspection of the room to address the audience. SHE holds a small paper French flag in one hand and an American flag in the other.*

GERTRUDE. Come in, come in! Welcome to 5 Rue Christine! Yes, Paris has been liberated, and the two of us are back where we belong. We haven't had time yet to have cards printed up, so I'll just tell you: Miss Gertrude Stein and Miss Alice B. Toklas are once more receiving visitors at home.

(*ALICE enters, carrying a desk drawer full of papers and photos.*)

GERTRUDE. Alice, we are really home at last!
ALICE. (*Putting drawer down on table, and putting out cigarette, which SHE has also been carrying in her hand.*)

Yes, though it will not seem so to me until I put things right. If I had known the Germans would ransack every drawer while we were shut away in Culoz, I would not have agreed to go.

GERTRUDE. Then it is well you did not know.

ALICE. Look at this, all our papers and photographs, tossed in a hopeless jumble ...

GERTRUDE. The important things are here. The pictures—

ALICE. Gertrude, they have stolen my petit point footstool. How dare they! With the design Pablo did for me. Somewhere, at this very moment, a huge, thickset, thick-headed German is resting his heavy boots on a priceless work of art.

GERTRUDE. Perhaps it will improve his mind, an infusion of culture from the bottom up. Alice, Paris is liberated, *we* are liberated. (*SHE regards her own portrait on the wall.*) And the treasures of our youth, the pictures and the drawings are saved.

ALICE. And I am saved. (*To the audience.*) Four years without a decent cigarette, that was the worst. It was so kind of that American journalist who called on us today—Eric ... Severeid—to offer me army rations. Under ordinary circumstances, I should have accepted happily, but it seemed greedy to take both food and cigarettes, so I had to decide. If he had not had Lucky Strikes, I might have favored the food. (*To Gertrude.*) Lucky Strikes! Since 1940 I have smoked such whimsical things—anything that could be dried and rolled into cigarette paper.

GERTRUDE. Except fig leaves.

ALICE. Well, naturally except fig leaves. Smoking fig leaves poisoned Maurice.

GERTRUDE. That was never clearly established.

ALICE. What else could it have been? These past four years, Gertrude, there have been no mysterious culprits. Everything we have eaten has been spare in quantity and easily identified.

GERTRUDE. (*Picking up a cookbook.*) Do you include the paper feasts?

ALICE. The paper—? *(SHE notices the cookbook.)* Delicious! Entirely perfect.

GERTRUDE. Pussy, you amazed me. Sitting there, reading cookbooks, evening after hungry evening throughout the long war. Such salacious delight you took in the triumphs of the French chefs.

ALICE. Their pale lobster bisques, their black truffle salads ...

GERTRUDE. Described in heartless black and white detail.

ALICE. During a war, one must be a bit like a camel, living on one's past. I thought of the war as a kind of perpetual Lent.

GERTRUDE. Observed by two Jewish ladies in their later years. Now that it is over, do you think we made a mistake, as everyone insisted, spending the war in France?

ALICE. (*To the audience.*) Gertrude's position on that did not leave room for argument. (*To Gertrude.*) "Here we are and here we stay," you said, and you were right. It was the correct arrangement. As you told them, "It is better to continue in a regular manner than to go irregularly where no one can help us if we are in trouble." That is certainly the analysis of a genius, which is, after all, what you are. (*SHE exits and returns during Gertrude's next speech, carrying an elaborately frosted fruitcake concealed beneath a dome.)*

GERTRUDE. Yes, that is what I am. And I had the good fortune also to be the youngest in my family, which means I have been accustomed to buffering. If you are a genius and the youngest as well, everyone must simply take care of you. In a war, buffering is of course a particular advantage. Being an eldest child, you had different expectations, which probably explains the fruitcake.

ALICE. Does it? My liberation fruitcake?

GERTRUDE. Yes, I believe so. In 1940, at the first sign of danger—

ALICE. It was hardly the first sign. But it had been, you know, so slow.

GERTRUDE. Alice, even a slow catastrophe is quite fast. Now, if I were to consider a future fruitcake as a distraction from catastrophe—but the idea is simply impossible. I was the youngest child in my family, accustomed to being taken care of, and I am still that youngest grown large. Therefore, I would never take it upon myself to fill two enormous glass jars—

ALICE. I had to, so I would have the right ingredients when the war was over.

GERTRUDE. —with pounds and pounds of citron and candied orange and lemon peel, and pounds more—

ALICE. I am sure there were not more than five or six pounds.

GERTRUDE. —of pineapple and cherries and raisins—

ALICE. The total was well under ten pounds.

GERTRUDE. —guarding and protecting those two glass jars for four long war years, burying them in the cellar by night when our house was billeted by German soldiers, refusing to trade them for flour or butter. We sold paintings just to buy the basics. We ate quite a good Cezanne rather than touch the ingredients of your liberation fruitcake.

ALICE. Do you think then, it was not a good idea?

GERTRUDE. Not at all, I think it was a superb idea, as are all of your ideas. I have been talking only about the ways of seeing things.

ALICE. The fruitcake was more important than butter. It was hope.

GERTRUDE. I know, your monument to survival. Or should I say your celebration of survival?

ALICE. That is closer to the truth. And to the colors.

GERTRUDE. Ah, the colors. Even if there were no fruitcake—

ALICE. But there is most definitely a fruitcake. (*SHE removes the dome and reveals it.*) I baked it this very morning, and iced it with one inch of almond paste, and tomorrow I shall send it to General Alexander Patch, with our sincere thanks for liberating the region of Bugey.

GERTRUDE. I only mean that the idea of your fruitcake is the important thing. It has been in your glass jars for four years, that *essential* fruitcake. That is the truth that Pablo and I discovered years ago, when the twentieth century was new, and almost everyone was still stuck in the nineteenth century. I understood it from the first, yet it wasn't until I flew in an airplane—

ALICE. (*To the audience.*) Back in America in 1934.

GERTRUDE. From the airplane I saw what Pablo and Cezanne and Braque had seen from the ground—the whole idea of cubism. Just like the parts of Pablo's violins and vases—and your fruitcake.

ALICE. Compositions do not just happen, as you well know. Arrangements must be *made,* and someone must make them.

GERTRUDE. Is that what you are doing now, with that pile of photographs?

ALICE. Yes, I am arranging our friends. Not for the first time.

GERTRUDE. (*Looking over Alice's shoulder.*) Ah, Ernest.

ALICE. I'm afraid so. And causing trouble as usual.

GERTRUDE. Alice, how can you say that? We haven't seen him for years.

ALICE. It's the wives.

GERTRUDE. Indeed. That is so often the case.

ALICE. Mr. Severeid told me, (*To the audience.*) just as I was ecstatically lighting my first Lucky Strike, that Ernest Hemingway has married again. (*To Gertrude.*) That makes number three.

GERTRUDE. And why should that trouble us?

ALICE. Sooner or later, we will receive a letter. A letter and a photograph of Ernest and his new wife.

GERTRUDE. Yes?

ALICE. And it will fall to me to arrange it, along with the photographs of the other two. Don't you see how it will crowd the page?

GERTRUDE. You have always been very clever at arranging for the wives.

ALICE. It was a rule, if I recall correctly. Your rule.

GERTRUDE. Sometimes they are necessary.

ALICE. That time, when you were trying to convince me to write my autobiography, you suggested several titles. Do you remember doing that?

GERTRUDE. I remember mainly that you ignored all my suggestions, and would not write a word, so that finally I had to write *The Autobiography of Alice B. Toklas* myself. (*SHE picks up the autobiography and looks through it with obvious satisfaction.*)

ALICE. Well the one title that tempted me, the one that almost got me writing was *Wives of Geniuses I Have Sat With*. I thought myself quite an authority on that subject. (*To the audience.*) You know Hadley, Ernest's first wife, never was a tea drinker before coming with him to see us at our old place at 27 Rue de Fleurus. Oh, I used to watch her like a hawk, watching Gertrude and Ernest, trying to find a literary crack in which to insert herself. Every time she opened her mouth to speak, I'd refill her cup and ask her once again whether it was one lump of sugar or two.

GERTRUDE. (*To the audience.*) Alice was magnificent. Always.

ALICE. I did what was required. But one thing I never fully understood, Gertrude. How did you know, when you sent them off for me to entertain, that none of the *wives* were geniuses?

GERTRUDE. I expect you would have told me if they were.

ALICE. It is a wonder, is it not, how many old friends managed to find us in Culoz, exiled as we were?

GERTRUDE. Oh, not exiled. Temporarily rearranged, perhaps.

ALICE. It was exile enough, living between the cliffs and the railway track, a million miles from Paris. (*To the audience.*) Such a huge, pretentious house in the middle of nowhere, inundated with goats.

GERTRUDE. Oh, the goats! That is how I knew we

were living in a castle.

ALICE. That is how?

GERTRUDE. Every day, the goats came out as we came in. That is real cordiality. (*To the audience.*) There are so many castles—some are built like castles, some are just called castles, and some are really castles. And those that are really castles always have something or someone coming in and going out. Always.

ALICE. For such a long time it seemed that very little came in. It was all paper feasts, consumed with gusto, but very low in calories.

GERTRUDE. That was not all! (*To the audience.*) We had our bread rations, and we learned to fish in the clever peasant fashion, with an open umbrella festooned with bait from every prong. And each day Alice performed another miraculous multiplication of loaves and fishes that left me awestruck. (*To Alice.*) We did not starve, thanks to you we did not.

ALICE. No thanks, certainly, to all those German soldiers who took possession of our house. *They* came in the castle, all right.

GERTRUDE. Getting them to go out of the castle was another matter. And their manners were perfectly dreadful. (*To the audience.*) One day I did ask them to go.

ALICE. (*Astonished and indignant.*) What an interesting suggestion. You asked the German soldiers, billeted in our house, to *go*? How did that come about?

GERTRUDE. I spoke only to the officer in charge. I was quite respectful of protocol.

ALICE. (*Barely able to control herself.*) Gertrude, for two years I had been carefully composing our portraits. (*To the audience.*) Two widowed French ladies of sixty-odd years, Catholic of course, with the right political views, living quietly in the countryside. (*To Gertrude.*) While you were composing *your* fictions, I was composing another set—for the two of us!

GERTRUDE. (*To the audience.*) It occurred one morning after breakfast. Alice had gone outside to tend the vegetable garden.

ALICE. You were supposed to be in your study, writing!

GERTRUDE. (*To the audience.*) It was the day they slaughtered the calf on the terrace. I said to the major, "It is time now," and pointed to the door.

ALICE. Gertrude, we are both Jewish!

GERTRUDE. I didn't see a need to mention that.

ALICE. (*With exaggerated patience over helpless rage.*) What happened? When you told him to leave.

GERTRUDE. (*Genuinely mirthful at the recollection.*) He thought I was pointing to the bathroom, that I was telling him it was free so he could take his bath! He clicked his heels, thanked me, and marched off.

ALICE. (*Caustically.*) I guess one doesn't argue with a genius.

GERTRUDE. I called after him, "Clean the tub when you are finished. Madame Toklas is quite particular about that." Truly, their manners were atrocious.

ALICE. It was my job to talk with them. You should have been in your study writing.

GERTRUDE. (*Still blithely unaware.*) Yes, you seemed to be always sending me off with my manuscript.

ALICE. (*To the audience, with very intense feeling.*) I have always protected—(*SHE stops herself, and finishes very quietly.*) Gertrude's writing schedule.

GERTRUDE. (*After a long pause, with full recognition.*) Yes, that is completely true. For more than thirty-five years, the arrangements have been all your doing.

(There is a moment's pause involving a shared acknowledgement.)

ALICE. Quite honestly, Gertrude, I think I shall never forgive the Germans for sneaking off with my footstool while we were away.

GERTRUDE. Probably you won't.

ALICE. And look at this will you? (*SHE lifts up a pile of photographs.*) All lumped together, and half of them aren't even speaking to each other. Pablo with three different mistresses, Matisse, Isadora Duncan, and Ernest and his first two wives. Now Gertrude, I ask you, wouldn't that make them all just livid?

End of Scene 2

ACT II

Scene 3

Wobblies by Carolyn Myers

CHARACTERS

ROSA LOWENSTEIN: In her eighties, a widow, and determined to achieve peaceful senility, Rosa has just this very day signed into the senior home. Rosa works hard to maintain her thin veneer of sweet-little-old-ladyhood, but right beneath the surface she is a feisty, sarcastic, and clever New Yorker with decades of radical political action behind her.

EMMA VANDEVERE: Rosa's comrade and sometimes leader, Emma, is at least eighty, blind, a longtime widow, and always a schemer. She has been in the senior home for some time, and is very discontented. Emma combines her political views with a love of risk- taking and a ribald sense of humor.

TIME & PLACE

Early summer, in the recent past, around 1985.
The recreation room of an institutional convalescent home near New York City.

SETTING: The dull, drab recreation room of an institutional senior home can be represented by as little as two horrible plastic chairs, placed side by side, directly facing the audience.

AT RISE: ROSA and EMMA sit in two chairs, close together, facing straight ahead. EMMA leans on her long cane, a blind cane, and ROSA holds a small paper cup and pills. ROSA is intending to take her medication.

ROSA. Cheers!

(ROSA begins to take her medication, but is intercepted by EMMA, who grabs the pills and cup, and throws them over her shoulder onto the floor.)

EMMA. Mustn't take that stuff, Rosa dear. Bad for little old ladies. Makes you dull as dishwater, slow as a tortoise, dizzy as a dust storm, limp as a rag, quiet as a lamb, good as gold—

ROSA. But I want to be quiet as a lamb and good as gold.

EMMA. What I want to tell you is, you can't take your medication because ... (*Although SHE can't see, SHE looks around conspiratorially and moves her chair closer and says in a whisper.*) I got a plan!

ROSA. A plan? On no, Emma Vandevere, you can just count me out of any plan you've got.

EMMA. But Rosa, listen. I've got it all set. I can't do it all alone, though. I can't see too good.

ROSA. You can't see at all. You are completely blind, Emma.

EMMA. Well, that's blunt. Anyway, then, like a miracle, if I believed in miracles, which I don't, you got committed here—

ROSA. Enrolled, Emma. Not committed. One gets enrolled in a nursing home. One gets committed to an asylum or to jail.

EMMA. Yeah? (*Pause.*) Anyway, I got this plan, see—

ROSA. No.

EMMA. You haven't even heard it yet.

ROSA. For fifty years, Emma Vandevere, I followed you around, one plan to the next, one demonstration to the next, my house an open house to every Commie in New York, the Red Hotel, Sammy used to call it. Now I am old, eighty years old, and I got my own plan.

EMMA. You do?

ROSA. And that's to sit right here and enjoy the view.

EMMA. For the rest of your life?

ROSA. (*In a very old voice, resigned.*) Such as it is.

EMMA. But, Rosie.

ROSA. (*Forgetting to be tired, jumping up and yelling.*) I'm tired, Emma. (*Remembering to be old, sitting down again and picking at her shawl.*) My strength is just not what it used to be.

EMMA. You're not tired. You're faking it, Mrs. Lowenstein.

ROSA. I just want to sit and rock.

EMMA. Sit and rot, you mean.

ROSA. Let my mind rest.

EMMA. Let your mind go, you mean.

(ROSA leans back and closes her eyes, settling in for a snooze. SHE hums sweetly to herself.)

EMMA. Well, if you're going to sit and rock, can I sing you a lullaby?
ROSA. Sing.
EMMA. Now, since you are my favorite Rose in all the world, I believe I will sing you my favorite Rose song.
ROSA. Lovely.
EMMA. *(SHE sings loud and off-key.)* "Oh, the yellow Rose of Texas, that I have gone to see—"
ROSA. *(SHE jerks awake, annoyed and animated.)* Texas! Why are you singing to me about Texas?
EMMA. Such a big state to hate all of it.
ROSA. I told him, "You can go organize those oil workers all by yourself, Sammy Lowenstein. I'm not moving out to that big, flat, redneck place."
EMMA. Lonely women at gas stations staring at tumbleweeds.
ROSA. Open my mouth and I'd be shot.
EMMA. That's right.
ROSA. Do you blame me?
EMMA. You always knew your own mind, Rose.
ROSA. As if there wasn't enough to do right here in New York.
EMMA. That's what I mean, Rosie! Now, about my plan—
ROSA. *(SHE's jerked back to the present.)* You tricked me, you old fart. You got me all worked up.
EMMA. You had me so worried, Rose. You'd only

been here one day and already you were starting to vegetate.

ROSA. Vegetation, exactly. That's my plan.

(ROSA settles back and closes her eyes stubbornly. EMMA produces a letter from her pocket and waves it about.)

EMMA. I got a very interesting letter here from Nina, Rosa.

ROSA. Nina, your granddaughter Nina? The feminist?

EMMA. Nina's up in the woods, Seneca Falls.

ROSA. What's she doing up there?

EMMA. They got a big peace camp up there, near the air force base.

ROSA. In the woods?

EMMA. They're holding big demonstrations to protest—

ROSA. Oh, no you don't, I'm not listening to you! *(SHE covers her ears and begins to hum.)* Mmmmmmm—

EMMA. The nuclear base there.

ROSA. Yab away. I'm not listening.

EMMA. Nina sent me a picture of the demonstration.

ROSA. Let me see that. *(SHE grabs the picture.)* They're climbing the fence!

EMMA. To raid the base, to dance on the silos.

ROSA. Hold on, wait a minute. Are these all women?

EMMA. Seems so.

ROSA. Why do they do that? All women?

EMMA. I don't know. But I intend to find out all about it when—*(Pause. SHE draws the chair closer.)* I go there.

ROSA. Go there? You?

EMMA. Us, Rosa. Both of us.

ROSA. Now I know for a certainty that you are completely nuts.

EMMA. But, Rosie. It's so boring here. They keep the TV on all the time, nobody wants to talk about politics, the workers don't want to organize, there's nothing to do. And these girls up at Nina's camp, they could use our help.

ROSA. What help could you possibly be, Emma? You can't even take care of yourself.

EMMA. Yes, I can.

ROSA. Listen to me, Emma. Why are you here?

EMMA. Oh, who knows.

ROSA. It's just a simple question. I want an answer. Why, Emma, why?

EMMA. Because I can't see so good.

ROSA. You can't see at all!

EMMA. Because I can't see so good and they won't let me live in my own place.

ROSA. You might forget to turn off the gas, you might fall on your face, right?

EMMA. Well—

ROSA. You might break your nose, you might break your hip, you might kill yourself, right?

EMMA. Well—

ROSA. Why are you here, Emma? Why are we both here? Because we cannot safely be any other place is why!

EMMA. No, that can't be true. Not alone maybe. Not anymore. But together we got two good minds. I'm only talking about a vacation, Rose. Just a little vacation to Seneca Falls. We're not moving there.

ROSA. Here they take care of us. We're warm, we're well fed.

EMMA. Well fed? Mashed potatoes Monday, tapioca

Tuesday ... Give up food. Give up chewing, give up tasting, give up life.

ROSA. Now you listen to me. You've got a daughter and I've got a daughter, right?

EMMA. That's right. Worse luck.

ROSA. My daughter says to me, "Mother ..." I don't know why she said it that way, she never calls me mother. Sounds like I'm some stranger. "Mother," she said, "Mother, we love you very much." She kept forming these words very slowly with her mouth. "Mother, we love you very much and we worry about you. Mother," my daughter says, "you can't go on living by yourself."

EMMA. And you believed her? This is no place for people who can think.

ROSA. My daughter is a certified public accountant.

EMMA. Oh Rosa, no! What a disappointment. Look at us, five kids between us and what have we got?

ROSA. Two lawyers and a CPA.

EMMA. And I've got a banker and a doctor—but don't get your hopes up. He has a very elite clientele, they pay him a lot of money for nothing, God forbid he should ever actually help someone. Our kids, finks, all of them. Not one of them has ever gone to jail for something they believed in, not one of them is even a social worker or a weird Buddhist or anything *real*. All they do is succeed. They worship money. Oh, Rosa, Rosa, where did we go wrong?

ROSA. Still, my daughter the CPA is very practical. I would not expect her to advise me in ways that were frivolous or thoughtless ... now, heartless perhaps.

EMMA. Rosa, what's happened to you? Me, I can explain. I'm visually impaired, that gave my kids a chance to sneak up on me. But you, there's nothing wrong with you. You just gave up.

ROSA. Well, ever since Sammy died—

EMMA. Oh horse manure. You always had twice the brains and guts Sammy did.

ROSA. *(ROSA is furious. SHE grabs Emma's cane and starts hitting her with it.)* You take that back, Emma! You just take that back! Sammy was a wonderful man.

EMMA. (*SHE grabs back cane.*) Okay, jeez, I didn't mean anything.

ROSA. Just don't talk to me anymore, Emma Vandevere. (*ROSA turns away.*)

(There's a short silence. Then EMMA giggles.)

EMMA. Three old women were sitting around talking. The first said, "My Peter, he bought me a mink coat." The second said, "My Dickie, he took me on a cruise in the Caribbean." The third said, "My John, he has a wang so long that twelve bluebirds can sit on it at once."

ROSA. (*Still turned away.*) We were both of us lucky in our men.

EMMA. The first old woman sighs and says, "Well, to tell the truth, that fur coat? It was really just a stole, and it was fake." The second old woman says, "That cruise? Actually just a fishing trip to Florida, and I only went for part of it."

(There's a short silence.)

ROSA. (*Turns back.*) Yeah?
EMMA. What do you mean, "Yeah?"

GIRL TALK

ROSA. That's it? That's the end of the joke?
EMMA. Yes, that's it, I think.
ROSA. Some joke.
EMMA. So I guess your daughter got your driver's license?
ROSA. Of course not! Why should she?
EMMA. "Because we worry about you, Mother."
ROSA. I passed my driving test. I got my pride.
EMMA. Yes, but do you have your license?
ROSA. I hid it.
EMMA. Where?
ROSA. I'm not telling.
EMMA. The third little old woman smiles and says ...
ROSA. Yes? What does she say, Emma?
EMMA. Where's that license?
ROSA. Oh, all right. Here it is.

(ROSA reaches into her bosom and pulls out her license. SHE hands it over to EMMA, who pockets it.)

EMMA. All right! The third little old woman smiles and says, "That twelfth bluebird, he could only get one foot on."

(THEY both laugh.)

EMMA. Now Rose, we got a lot of planning to do.
ROSA. We better go to my room. No one should hear.

(THEY stand and start to leave.)

ROSA. You got to admit, I tried to sink into a

doddering dotage.

EMMA. You gave it the old leftist try, all right.

ROSA. All my life I worked hard.

EMMA. You deserve a rest, it's true.

ROSA. I couldn't dodder at home, either. People kept calling me up, life kept calling me up. Even the night before I got—committed—here, when all I wanted was to stay at home and play with my ghosts, I got called up to go to a demonstration.

EMMA. You never could resist a demonstration, Rose.

ROSA. Boy, did my daughter hate that.

EMMA. She wants you to be a foolish old woman. She wants to take over.

ROSA. It's the least I could do for her. I've been a very upsetting mother in every other way.

EMMA. So you came here, just like she wanted you to.

ROSA. And immediately try to escape.

EMMA. It's not an escape. We're not in jail.

ROSA. Then why don't we walk out the front door?

EMMA. You've got a point.

ROSA. My daughter is going to be so upset.

EMMA. She's young. She'll get over it.

ROSA. She's not young. She's nearly sixty.

EMMA. She'll get over it, Rose, she'll get over it.

(THEY begin to walk off together.)

END OF PLAY

COSTUMES

In the original production, in which the same two actresses played all roles, minimal costume effects were added to basic costumes of simple skirts and tops. These were displayed on coat racks positioned upstage right and left, and changes were made in full view of the audience. The following list focuses on character attributes which should be kept in mind when designing costumes for Girl Talk.

Rites of Passage
Jenny: Feminine teen attire—something special for this important day.
Georgie: Athletic teen attire

Grace Under Pressure
Grace: Eccentric, colorful "at-home" wear.

The Unmapped Way
Mary: 1915 party dress
Mabel: Shawl and hat, 1915 party dress (more simple than Mary's)
(In minimal plan, two shawls, plus a hat for Mabel will suffice)

Tick-Tock
Judy: Kimono or bathrobe
Liz: Casual clothes

True Stories
Leila: Relaxed clothing, with a sense of sophistication and

elegance.

Arrangements
Gertrude: Tweed skirt, silk or cotton shirt, tailored vest
Alice: Dark dress or ensemble worn with spectacular, large earrings
(In the original production, Gertrude added a vest to her basic costume, and Alice covered hers with a smock.)

Wobblies
Emma: Pants and sweater or sweatshirt, which need not go well together, and a cane.
Rosa: Similar to above, but clothes should appear newer and more carefully selected than Emma's. Rosa also wears a shawl, and her sweater is decorated with political buttons.

PROPERTIES

Rites of Passage
School books, notebooks, hand mirror (For Jenny)
School books, notebook with untidy papers slipping out (for Georgie)

Grace Under Pressure
Telephone
Tea pot with tea
Sugar bowl
Creamer
Cup and saucer
Teaspoon
Pad of paper
Pen
Crumpled piece of paper
Napkin (for mopping up spilled tea)

The Unmapped Way
Painting, covered by a cloth
Easel
A few pieces of Indian memorabilia, including a small bag of herbs
Cut flowers
Vase
Old diary

Tick-Tock
Coffee pot with coffee
Two mugs

True Stories
Books and papers
Vase of flowers
Hand mirror
One or two small, attractive art objects

Arrangements
Reproduction of Picasso's famous portrait of Gertrude Stein
(An inexpensive poster of this painting is available from the Metropolitan Museum of Art, New York)
Small paper
French flag
Small paper
American flag
Desk drawer containing black and white photographs
Cigarette case with standard length cigarettes
Ashtray
Matches
Fruitcake with thick frosting resembling almond paste
Dome-covered cake plate
Stacks of books, including several cookbooks, and one representing a First Edition of The Autobiography of Alice B. Toklas

Wobblies
Cane, preferably a blind cane
Small paper cup with water
Several pills
Envelope holding letter and snapshot
Driver's license

SET PIECES

Girl Talk can be performed with as little as one table and two chairs. In the original production, a tall, rattan étagère, upstage center, provided shelves for props, and two bentwood coat racks for costumes were positioned upstage right and left. More elaborate productions might include a variety of appropriate furnishings, such as a settee for Mary and Mabel in "The Unmapped Way," a writing table for Leila in "True Stories," and easy chair for Gertrude in "Arrangements," and institutional-looking chairs for Rosa and Emma in "Wobblies."

I STAND BEFORE YOU NAKED
by Joyce Carol Oates
Monologues

(Little Theatre) 11f. (doubling possible—original production was done with 6f.) Bare stage. This extraordinary new collection of dramatic monologues by one of America's foremost novelists, poets, essayists and women of letters rivals *Talking With* in dramatic intensity, language and sheer weirdness. The evening begins and ends with the title poem, a haunting evocation of Woman on the edge of the madness of vulnerability. There is humor here, but mostly the monologues grip us in the firm hold of a master writer interested more in the pathetic, the strange, the horrifying. In other words, this is vintage Joyce Carol Oates. Contains the following monologues: "Little Blood Button," "Wife of," "Wealthy Lady," "The Boy," "The Orange," "Good Morning, Good Afternoon," "Darling, I'm Telling You (Angel Eyes)," "Nuclear Holocaust," "Slow Motion," "Pregnant." **(#11681)**

VITAL SIGNS
by Jane Martin
Monologue play

(Little Theatre) 2m., (optional), 6f. Bare stage. The mysterious, pseudonymous Louisvillian, author of the acclaimed *Talking With,* has never been funnier, or more dramatically compelling, than in this extraordinary suite of theatrical miniatures, over thirty monologues with a length of around two minutes each, for six actresses. The two men in the play are "foils" for these compelling women. Although they do speak in one piece, their presence in your cast may be optional. Somehow, all the pieces add up to a collage of contemporary woman in all her warmth and majesty, her fear and frustration, her joy and her sadness. *Vital Signs* wowed them at the Humana Festival at Actors Theatre of Louisville, where its exciting first production was staged by Artistic Director Jon Jory. Included in our book are the details of Mr. Jory's direction which kept the theatrical ball rolling, headed into the pocket for a strike. "It does not just celebrate language from colorful women; [it] does the hoe-down."—Detroit Free Press. The New York Times praised "the continuing vitality and originality of the author's voice." "Offers wonderful opportunities for actresses to show off their versatility."—Washington Times. "Martin's eye and ear for the texture of everyday life in this culture is as playfully accurate as Lily Tomlin and Jane Wagner's. She's a fine quipster; but she manages, too, to open little windows of sadness into women's souls."—Detroit News. **(#24019)**